TO THE BIGGEST LITTLE PLANE LOVERS WE KNOW.

The Little Plane That Could

Published by Flying Thru Life Publications 2020

Text Copyright@2020
Susan Gilbert & Robert DeLaurentis
Illustrations Copyright@2020 ER Croft

Printed in the USA.

All inquiries should be directed to:
www.FlyingThruLife.com

ISBN-13: 978-1-7324937-1-1

THE LITTLE PLANE THAT COULD

written by:
Susan Gilbert and Robert DeLaurentis
illustrated by:
Eddie Croft

A small red plane sits in a hangar pointed towards

the runway and watches planes take off and land.

NNNEEAOOWWW!

Nnneeaoowww

is the sound of propeller planes flying overhead.

This small red plane is young and not yet able to fly.

He dreams about when he will be ready to make

circles in the sky like the big planes.

His name is

Dash watches the planes take off and land.

Dash sighs, "When will it be my turn?"

Then he remembers.

Soon I will be able to join them.

That's what the elders - the full size and bigger

planes - tell him. He waits and dreams of that day,

wondering if he really could fly like them.

Dash is growing bigger and bigger every day.

He has his wings.

He has his two legs with wheels attached at the ends.

Next, he will get a special addition to his nose.

On an airplane, the nose has a propeller that spins.

While Dash waits, he watches the other planes at the airport from his home which is called a hangar.

DASH IS RED

Planes can be any color.

"Look at that yellow one lift off quickly and disappear into the clouds!" Dash said excitedly.

He sees so many different colors roll past his hanger on their way to the runway for takeoff.

When planes roll slowly along the ground before takeoff or after landing it is called taxiing.

Planes can be many different shapes and sizes.
They all have a body, wings and at least one propeller.
Except for jet planes.

Some plane wings are high above their body
and others are even or below their body.

Some even have **2** sets of wings.

Dash is happy with his **1** set of wings.

Soon he will be able to use them. He dreams of that
day and believes that one day he, too, will be able to fly.

His mother reminds him every day that he will.

Big planes, little planes and different

colored planes come and go.

Planes land.

Planes take off.

Dash watches the planes on the runway

day after day from his hanger.

Dash waits for his turn.

Day after day. Waiting. Waiting.

"When will it be my turn?" Dash asks.

Dash's favorite part of the day is when the airplanes who live

at his airport gather together at the end of the day when the

sunlight fades and night begins. They tell stories of where

they have flown. One by one they roll into the hangar,

nod hello to each other and form a circle.

Dash puts on his favorite pajamas covered in red polka dots.

For Dash, it's almost bedtime.

He is excited to hear the elder planes tell their stories.

SAMMY SPITFIRE

the oldest plane in the circle of planes, and the most respected

elder of the group, begins to speak.

The hangar fills with silence,

each plane waiting to hear what Sammy will say.

Sammy begins,

"I was created to fly higher and faster and protect the pilots who

flew with me so that they became the heroes of the sky."

Rosie, Dash's mother nods while looking at Sammy and says,

"We thank you for your brave service."

says,

"Sammy was built to fly high and fast.

I was built to fly low and slow.

You should see what I can do with my two pairs of wings!

I get to fly above the cornfields, pastures, and farms.

I enjoy looking down at the countryside, and up at the sky.

I can fly with the breeze!"

Barney exclaims.

Another plane rolls into the hangar to join the elder circle.

"I'd like to introduce myself. I'm

LARRY LONG-DISTANCE

I am returning from a long flight across the

Atlantic Ocean, where I flew over Africa.

Would you like to hear about what I saw there?"

All the planes nodded their noses in unison saying,

YES!

"I flew above the red sand dunes of Namibia.

I flew over the open jungles and rivers of Botswana.

I saw elephants, giraffes…below me."

Larry Long-Distance continued, "I could see
many families traveling together.

Lions with their cubs. Elephants both big and small."

Rosie tucks her wing around Dash's

small body and pulls him close.

Looking down at him she says, "Look at all the

adventures you can have, Dash.

When you are big enough, you will no longer

live only on the ground.

You will fly higher and farther each time you practice and

you will learn how to fly over rivers, plains and mountains.

You will see the fields that Barney told us about and

the foreign lands like Africa that Larry has seen."

As the moon rises high in the sky and the stars sparkle

brightly, Rosie turns to the elders and Dash and says,

"Thank you all for coming together here tonight

and sharing your flying stories.

Now it's time for us to return to our homes

and rest for tomorrow."

Turning to Dash, she says, "Follow me and I'll make

sure you are tucked in for the night.

It's important you get a good night's sleep."

The next morning arrives with clear blue skies.

Rosie rolls over to Dash, smiles and greets him,

"Good morning! Today is a very important day.

We knew the time would come and I'll bet you

are surprised it happened so quickly.

You've done well in school. It's time to get your

propeller installed so you can take your first flight."

Dash's eyes pop open wide.

He is so excited! It's finally time to fly!

Dash had thought about this day.

Dash had dreamed about this day.

And finally, today is the day!

The mechanic fastens Dash's shiny nose into place.

Dash looks at his reflection in the glass window

and admires his new nose. It is a fine nose propeller.

Dash's mother rolls towards him smiling.

He could tell she likes his nose, too.

But now he wonders, "Can I really fly?"

The next morning, just like every morning,

he goes to Flight School. Dash studies his lessons.

He is doing so well that his teacher says he'll be able graduate.

DASH IS EXCITED!

And scared!

He has his new propeller.

He is a good student in school.

But can he really fly?

The next morning is a very big day!

Dash graduates from Flight School.

Dash's mother waves him toward her with her wing,

motioning for him to follow her out to the runway.

And then he knew...

IT IS TIME TO FLY.

He's been waiting for this day his whole life!

Dash's teacher, Buzz, is there so he isn't alone.

Following Buzz's instructions, Dash takes his

position on the runway's center line.

He is scared but doesn't want to show it.

He starts rolling faster and faster down the runway.

Just like he learned in school.

FASTER AND FASTER

so he can lift off into the sky and fly.

But then…

Dash begins to slow down on the runway.

He stops. He thinks to himself, "Can I really fly?"

Then he remembers, "I am made for this!

I may be small, but I have all the necessary parts now.

I have my propeller.

I went to school to learn how to fly.

I am ready to make everything work together.

Yes, I can fly!"

Starting again, Dash begins rolling faster

and faster down the runway.

It isn't long before the wind

under his wings lifts him into the air.

He did it! He is flying!

As he flies higher up into the sky,

he looks down at the airport with all the

planes watching him from the ground.

All of them are cheering for him.

Dash knows this is just the beginning

of many adventures to come.

After all,

he is finally...

THE LITTLE PLANE THAT COULD!

THE END

About the Authors

Susan Gilbert read many books that made her want to fly, just like Dash. The time finally came when she took flying lessons and sitting inside a small plane just like Dash, took to flying circles in the air.

Robert DeLaurentis dreamed of flying since his childhood; building planes of paper, balsa wood and plastic. As a pilot, he has circled the globe twice in his own small aircraft: "Spirit of San Diego" & "Citizen of the World".

A Word from the Authors

If you enjoyed this book, please take time to leave a friendly review on Amazon, as your kind feedback is very appreciated and important to us. Good reviews give the authors, illustrator and potential readers encouragement on stormy days that keep us on the ground.

Thank you!

Made in the USA
Monee, IL
24 December 2020